Deep Breathing Exercises for Anxiety

Discover How To Reduce Anxiety With These 6 Simple Breathing Exercises

by Angira Lisbon

Table of Contents

Introduction

Are you suffering from anxiety? Do you feel over-stressed for most of your day? Does it seem like the little things in life unbalance your calm and get to you more easily now? Or have you tried breathing exercises before but found them ineffective?

Stress, panic, and anxiety are a part of daily modern life, and the longer they are ignored, the worse they become. While some people are lucky enough to find their own internal calm, most just pretend to be fine until these problems lead to graver health issues like heart complications, respiratory disorders, or panic attacks.

Oftentimes, you find yourself in stressful situations where relaxing through external means just isn't practical or feasible. Advice from experts telling you to "keep yourself calm" is about as useful as a plastic spoon when fighting an alligator. So what can you do to help yourself without the need to seclude yourself from your stress-inducing surroundings? If you've tried such exercises before, and found that they don't work, what are you doing wrong?

That is precisely the *raison d'être* of this guide. I'm going to guide you through exercises that can be done immediately, quietly, and on the down-low, without the need for anything other than regulating your own breathing.

If you wonder about the authenticity of such methods, or how to find time for them, don't worry, we'll clear up several misconceptions about why these methods won't work. After all, these exercises form the base of many spiritual philosophies, and several cultures throughout the civilized world absolutely swear by them. There's a reason for that. Simply put, these exercises are nothing short of effective.

So, are you ready to unlock the pathway to calm without the need for any feel-good pill-popping prescriptions or expensive therapies? Are you ready to learn the most basic and easiest of ways to beat anxiety through the regulation of your own inner peace? Let's get started!

Chapter 1: How Do Breathing Exercises Work Against Anxiety?

Many people – especially the ones who've been improperly trained or have half-baked knowledge on the matters – scoff at the idea of beating anxiety and stress through breathing exercises. However, scientific research has conclusively proven that breath regulation **does work** – irrespective of who does it and where. This is unlike the constant disclaimers on pharmaceutical therapies that claim that the same drugs could have different magnitudes of effectiveness on different people. How, then, do these exercises benefit their practitioners?

The human body has two major classifications under its nervous system: central and peripheral. Among other things, the peripheral nervous system also contains the autonomic nervous system, which controls the activity of organs, glands, and various involuntary muscles and functions of our body, like peeing yourself out of fear.

The autonomic nervous system contains two complementary systems: the sympathetic and parasympathetic nervous systems. Think of these two as twins, and contrary to the image that the names may conjure, the sympathetic nervous system is the hyper-caffeinated, over-hyped, constantly restless, and mischievous twin while the parasympathetic system is the one that has a calming effect and keeps its sibling from blowing itself up, as it were. The sympathetic nervous system is the part that deals with fight or flight impulses, and is responsible for more adrenalin secretion, accelerated pumping of the heart, and all those functions that are designed to keep your body going in times of emergency without keeling over from exhaustion. Unfortunately, all those nasty functions also make you feel like you're even more panicky, stressed, or anxious.

While it may be for a good reason, these responses are hardly helpful when you're already stressed out and need to relax more than anything else. This is where the parasympathetic system comes in, which smoothly kicks its over-hyper sibling in the fork of its legs and tells it to calm the hell down. It reduces adrenalin function, and basically brings your body out of emergency mode and into normal and relaxed functions.

The problem is – as the name should tell you – the autonomic systems are self-regulating, involuntary, and not really under our conscious control. So how can we activate the parasympathetic system when we need to relax and calm ourselves?

Whenever we are in a state of emergency or heightened activity, the message that's going from our respiratory organs to our brain is: I'm running out of air, I need more juice, make it happen pronto! But this same message is sent when we're over-stressed about something, which can lead to anxiety attacks or hyperventilation, which sends the same message again, even though that is the worst thing possible at the moment. Our bodies are a bit silly like that, we have a few bugs to iron out here and there.

Out of all the triggers that help control that involuntary system – which by definition is not under our control – the **only** thing that we can actively do at that point is to control our breathing to change the messages our body is sending. At such a time, regulating the depth and pattern of our breathing changes the signals being sent from our lungs to our brain, and results in innumerable biochemical reactions happening one after the other that end up releasing calming, anti-anxiety, or simply delicious chemicals like endorphins and their stress-whooping brethren.

Now that we've cleared up the issue of whether or not breathing exercises work against anxiety and stress, let's move on to time issues.

Chapter 2: I'm Too Busy – How to Find or Make Time

The most basic misconception that people have about such exercises is that they'll somehow cut into your busy schedule, when you already barely have any free time to take that long and relaxing bath you've been planning for weeks now.

Whenever people think of such methods, they seem to imagine images of yoga mats, incense sticks, oriental music, and hours of practice guided by a wise master sitting somewhere – or is that just me?

The truth of the matter is that these exercises can be smoothly integrated into your daily routine, rather than taking time away from them. As a matter of fact, I'm doing one of them right now because the thought of lawsuits over harmless jokes every time I write really stresses me out.

Even though the exercises that I'll write about in further chapters will mention seated positions or quiet atmospheres, those aren't requirements in any way to successfully complete the exercises and reap their benefits. You can do them anywhere – whether you're standing in a line, going grocery shopping, or doing the dishes – you're limited only by your imagination!

Lastly, don't think of these as exercises in the same manner most of us do when we need to go to the gym: Ugh, do I really need to? Instead, think of these as habits, which, once formed, can be summoned at a moment's notice to help you when you need them the most, or even to do when you have time to kill in the checkout line.

Like most exercises, the more you practice them, the better they work. Not only will this help you beat the pants off of anxiety when it rears its ugly head, it will keep you calmer the rest of the time as well.

Chapter 3: On the Spot Breathing Exercises When Faced With Anxiety

For the sake of maximizing benefits and understanding, I'm going to divide the exercises into two segments: stuff that will help you the most when you're severely anxious and hyperventilating, and stuff that will help you deal with general de-stressing and relief from everyday anxiety.

This chapter deals with the first kind. The main reason why I separate these criteria is that even though we *are* breathing when we're panicky, we're either breathing too fast for our body to actually absorb the oxygen that we need and so the breaths are wasted, or we're breathing in so much oxygen in those rapid breaths that we're getting dizzy and light headed from it (yes, that happens whether we have too much oxygen or too much carbon dioxide – guess your annoying doctors were right when they told you that too much of anything is bad). While there are plenty of exercises to go around, the trick is to recognize which one will work best for you and going with it.

Exercise 1: Using the Most of Your Breath

It's easy to understand which one of the situations that I discussed is being dealt with in this exercise.

15

You can perform this exercise absolutely anywhere, and don't need to be an Indian mystic-level expert to do this successfully, all you need to be able to do is count.

1. Close your eyes and mouth, with your lips shut but not tightly pressed together.

2. Relax your tongue so that it's resting against the bottom of your mouth, rather than pressed against the roof of your mouth or the inside of your top row of teeth. You'll immediately be able to sense how this relaxes your throat and opens up your airways.

3. Take in a deep breath through your nose, and count to four (1 Mississippi, 2 Mississippi, 3...) while you're breathing in. Make sure that you regulate the speed your breathing so that the inhalation lasts for the entire count. The more you practice this exercise, the further you can stretch the count – even comfortably going up to counts of 10 and further for more experienced practitioners.

4. Hold your breath for a count of four (1 Mississippi, 2 Mississippi, 3...). Regardless of however long you count for your inhalation, don't hold your breath for longer than a count of 7-10. This isn't a lung-training exercise. The slower you breathe in, the faster the air in your lungs goes stale, and the sooner you start feeling dizzy from lack of oxygen.

5. In a relaxed manner, slowly part your lips and exhale for a count of four though your mouth. Regulate your exhalation so that it lasts the entire count. Alternately, you can also just exhale through your nose, which helps you practice the exercise better since it offers more resistance to the flow of air (or you're trying to hide from a hit-man and don't want to make a sound).

6. Repeat the exercise for as long as it takes for you to start feeling less anxious. Keep your eyes closed through the exercise and concentrate on the sound and rhythm of your breathing.

The slow inhalation and exhalation ensures that your lungs get plenty of time to absorb the oxygen that they need, especially when you're in a situation of high anxiety when you need your brain to function.

Exercise 2: Re-breathing

This exercise is particularly useful when you feel like you're taking in plenty of deep breaths, yet can't seem to get any air into your lungs. You manage to exclaim that you can't breathe, and nothing you do seems to get that pressure off your chest. First, if you're talking, then you **are** breathing, since we talk by pushing air through our voice box and over our vocal chords to make sounds which are then shaped by our mouth and tongue.

The problem here is that you've breathed in too much oxygen, and even though your body has plenty of oxygen, you're still feeling dizzy as if your breath has been cut off. Your own panic is then sending you into a vicious cycle of breathing too hard to catch some air followed by your brain sending panicky signals since you still feel dizzy followed by further hard breathing to rectify that situation in your body and so on.

Instead, what you need is to bring up the carbon dioxide level in your bloodstream to bring you down from that oxygen high and help you normalize faster. While people use plastic and paper bags for this exercise, I'm going to assume that you don't have them at hand and proceed accordingly. Although, if you do have them, then use them since they do help a tad faster – but only by a tad, mind you.

1. Cup your hands over your mouth and nose. If you have a handkerchief or something in your pocket, you can use that in your hand to form a better seal. However, whatever you use, remember to cover your mouth and nose together, otherwise this is pointless.

2. Take a deep breath through your nose to the count of 6 Mississippi. The longer breath is to avoid you further worsening the situation by continuing to breathe at the same pace. If you feel like you can't regulate your pace of breathing, then proceed with the exercise at whatever pace your panic allows you till you feel you have regained at least some control.

3. Your panic may not allow you to hold your breath, so instead just exhale to the count of 6 Mississippi through your nose. Again, if you feel like you can't control it, then proceed at whatever pace you can till you regain some control.

4. As soon as you finish exhaling, inhale while holding your hand tightly over your mouth and nose. This should allow you to inhale back at least some of the carbon dioxide you just exhaled.

5. Whichever pace that you feel you can breathe at, continue the exercise till you start feeling more in control. Inhale directly after each exhalation without any pause so as to give yourself the best chance to breathe in more carbon dioxide. You need to recycle your stale air so that you can bring up your carbon dioxide levels faster without worsening the problem with more hyper-oxygenation. That's why a bag works better in such situations.

6. If you're prone to feeling this way from time to time, keep a paper or plastic bag with you in a pocket.

Chapter 4: Everyday Breathing Exercises to Prevent Stress and Anxiety

As opposed to the immediate and urgent physical needs that have been addressed in the chapter above, this one deals with everyday de-stressing or high anxiety. These exercises help you ward off the negative effects brought on by your everyday worries and tensions, stay calmer and more collected, prevent you from getting unbalanced by smaller issues, and improve your overall health.

Many of these breathing exercises have been used in disciplines such as yoga and meditation. Buddhists also use them to practice mindfulness: a concept which emphasizes paying attention to what's happening right now, rather than getting embroiled in future worries and imagined pains and failures. Mindfulness teaches us to drink in every sensation that we feel in and around us, and pay attention only to the very immediate present – from second to second – rather than stressing out about events that aren't under our immediate control or that haven't even occurred yet but the mere possibility of which is stressing us out.

These exercises – as I mentioned before – can be practiced anywhere and require no special setting or tool in order to be effective.

Exercise 1: Diaphragmatic Breathing Exercise

This exercise, in many parts of the world, is thought of as less of a general exercise to be performed under specific situations, and more as a general habit of breathing to be practiced and performed every day. It is also described as breathing through your belly or stomach, because that's the part of your body that seemingly inflates while breathing – even though that's so because it activates better functioning of your diaphragm, the ring of muscle separating the lower half of your torso from your rib cage and which is one of the muscles that help your lungs expand and contract better. You can use this exercise more freely as you gain more practice with it, by which I mean you can skip the first step once you get the hang of it.

1. Once you're seated comfortably (you don't need to sit cross-legged or on the floor, and can even do this on your favorite armchair or in bed as long as you're comfortable), close your eyes and keep one hand on your chest, while keeping the other hand on your stomach.

2. Inhale through your nose till the count of 5 Mississippi (for the sake of clarity, all further counts mentioned are Mississippi, if you get my drift), and push your stomach out as you breathe in. Your chest should barely rise or not rise at all. As you breathe in through your stomach, you'll find that drawing a deep breath is far easier this way than when your chest bulges out while inhaling. That's because your diaphragm gets more space to allow your lungs to

expand further. This increases the limits of how deeply your deep breaths can be.

3. Hold your breath for a count of 5.

4. Relax your lips slightly and exhale through your mouth, without need for a count but without any rush either, and this time pull your stomach in. You'll find that it takes far less effort to exhale by simply pulling your stomach in than by concentrating on your lungs during the exhalation. If you've only slightly parted your lips while exhaling, you'll be able to hear your breath exit your body. Concentrate on that sound during each exhalation, it'll let you focus on what you're doing and form the base for mindfulness.

5. Repeat the exercise for at least 15 minutes every day. Keep your eyes closed through the exercise and concentrate on the sound and rhythm of your breathing. With more practice, you'll find that you no longer need to keep track of your chest and stomach with your hands or close your eyes, and you'll be able to freely practice it anywhere and at any time.

Exercise 2: Kapalbhati

This is an old Yogic breathing exercise, and can be practiced every day at the start of your morning. Since this exercise is less subtle, it is best practiced indoors in a comfortable environment, and isn't one of the exercises that you can perform on the go. However, regular practitioners of Kapalbhati swear by its energizing properties, which help them keep themselves off of stimulants like coffee, and hence reduces their general stress and anxiety. Kapalbhati can be performed first thing in the morning in order to shake yourself off and launch yourself into a new day. It also strengthens your lungs – which helps manage your breathing better throughout the day and lowers stress triggers – as well as belly muscles, and so serves dual beneficial purposes. Kapalbhati is discussed here because it uses the fundamentals of breathing through one's stomach as its base.

1. Sit in a comfortable position (same stipulations as the previous exercise, and you might also want to keep a handkerchief with you – just in case), and close your eyes. You can rest one hand on your lap or your knee or leave it in a relaxed manner by your side. Place the other hand gently on your stomach.

2. Inhale through your nose for a count of 4.

3. Hold your breath for a count of 2.

4. Leaving your hand in a relaxed manner on your stomach, exhale in an explosive burst through your nose. You achieve this by quickly pulling your stomach in, as opposed to the long and relaxed exhalation of the previous exercise (now do you

understand the need for that just-in-case-handkerchief?).

5. Kapalbhati is then basically characterized by these long inhalations, followed by a short pause for preparation and an explosive exhalation. Repeat it for 10 to 15 minutes every day, and feel yourself shed that post-wakeup lethargy and grogginess aside without the need for any stimulants. Keep your eyes closed throughout the exercise and concentrate on the sound and rhythm of your breathing.

You can even perform this exercise twice a day, once in the morning and once in the evening, or whenever else after your morning routine that you may feel in the need of a pick-me-up.

Exercise 3: Nostril Regulation Breathing

Also called Nadi Shodhana, this is another exercise from the handbook of yogis, and is extremely effective as a calming and de-stressing tool. This is best performed in airy spaces, and is another exercise to add to your morning regimen. This exercise is also quite conspicuous and so can't be performed on the go. While it is traditionally performed while sitting cross-legged with a straight back, I've already mentioned that these exercises can be performed just as effectively in a setting that works best for you.

1. Close your eyes. Lift your right hand and hold it gently in front of your face. Hold your thumb and

25

little finger out as if it's an imaginary cell-phone, while closing the rest of your fingers. Press against the right side of your nose gently with your thumb so as to close that nostril, while holding your little finger out.

2. Inhale through your left nostril for a count of 5.

3. Press the pad of your little finger against the left side of your nose to close the left nostril. Your nose should now appear to be gently pinched between your thumb and little finger. Hold your breath for a count of 5.

4. Lift your thumb off the right side of your nose, and exhale slowly through your right nostril for a count of 5.

5. Keep your little finger pressed against the left side of your nose, and inhale through your right nostril for a count of 5 this time.

6. Close both your nostrils again as explained above, and hold your breath for another count of 5.

7. Lift your little finger off your nose, and exhale gently for a count of 5 through your left nostril.

8. Repeat this cycle for at least 10 – 15 minutes. Keep your eyes closed through the exercise and concentrate on the sound and rhythm of your breathing.

Exercise 4 – Visualized Breathing

This exercise requires a bit more visualization, and works best in calm surroundings. However, as long as you're not driving or performing any activity that requires immediate and unwavering focus, you can close your eyes for a few seconds or half a minute and practice it anywhere if you find yourself stressing out and needing to relax.

1. Close your eyes. In the darkness behind your closed eyes, imagine looking at yourself as a blank outline against a dark background. The only thing inside that outline should be an animated image of your brain. If you're angry, imagine your brain swathed in a fog of red gases, and if you're just stressed or anxious – imagine it as a black fog of gases swirling and filling inside your head.

2. While keeping your eyes closed, take in a deep breath through your nose to a count of 5. Breathe in through your stomach, as we've discussed before, rather than through your chest. Imagine the breath that you're taking as a green or blue colored gas, whichever color soothes you more. As you inhale, imagine that soothing gas rushing into your head instead of your lungs and mixing with the gas already there.

3. Instead of holding your breath, exhale slowly through your mouth for a count of 5. This time, imagine the other gas – red or black – being exhaled out instead. As you imagine that, feel your anger or stress slowly but perceptibly dropping little by little as it drains out of you. The aim here is to slowly replace that black or red gas inside your head with the soothing one that you inhale from all around you.

4. Keep repeating this exercise, and visualize that soothing green or blue gas replacing the darker ones in your head, till you've successfully replaced all of it for now and feel calmer and less stressed. Keep your eyes closed through the exercise and concentrate on the sound and rhythm of your breathing, along with the visualization. While this should take about 10 to 15 minutes when you first start practicing this exercise, slowly you'll be able to work yourself to a state where 30 seconds of it is enough to help you feel more relaxed – especially if you're outside and unable to devote 10 minutes to it.

While there are plenty more breathing exercises out there, the exercises that I've noted here require no previous training for breathing, and can be comfortably taken up by beginners. They will help you greatly in battling the demons of anxiety and stress, without needing any outside help for it.

Chapter 5: Breathing and Anti-Anxiety Aids and Applications

While you most definitely **do not** need outside tools or aids in order to practice these exercises, the beauty of modern technology is that there are plenty of helpful tools that you can carry around in your phone to help you increase their effectiveness – regardless of whether you use the Apple store or Android. Some of these provide calming music or soothing sounds to improve your environment, while others are guided meditation and breathing session apps, and others provide instructional or self-help videos for anxiety and stress management. Above all, these are all **FREE**.

Free Android Apps for help with guided meditation, breathing exercises or self-help videos

1. Anti-Anxiety App

2. Self-Help for Anxiety Management [SAM]

3. Relax Ocean Waves Sleep by Moz

4. Stop Panic & Anxiety Help

5. Worry Box

6. Nature Sounds Relax and Sleep

7. Breathe2Relax

8. Relax Melodies

9. Qi Gong Meditation Relaxation

10. Calming Music to Simplicity

11. Universal Breathing – Pranayama Free

Free Apple Apps for help with guided meditation, breathing exercises or self-help videos

1. Breathe2Relax

2. Self-Help for Anxiety Management [SAM]

3. Universal Breathing – Pranayama Free

4. Relaxing Sounds of Nature Lite

5. I Can Be Fearless by Human Progress

6. Anxiety Free

7. Relax Melodies

With these apps, you can enhance your breathing and meditation sessions, and carry your additional anxiety busters with you wherever you go.

Conclusion

While many people treat breathing exercises as a nuisance or a daunting task, the fact is that they are neither, and they come with a ton of benefits to boot even if you don't suffer from anxiety or stress disorders.

The fact remains that millions of people around the world today have developed various anxiety-related disorders, while billions more go through crippling anxiety on a daily basis from their environments alone. Ignoring these problems is no longer a luxury that we have, and why should we? Especially when all you need to do is breathe in and out – a task that you perform every minute of every day regardless.

Instead of trying to procrastinate or finding excuses for not delving into them, I would suggest going back up to the exercise section, finding one that interests you, and trying it out right away – even if you do it just for kicks!

I can assure you through personal experience that not only will these simple exercises help you beat anxiety, they will also help you find a calm center within yourself that will enrich and lighten your daily life like never before!

Finally, I'd like to thank you for purchasing this book! If you enjoyed it or found it helpful, I'd greatly appreciate it if you'd take a moment to leave a review on Amazon. Thank you!

Made in the USA
Middletown, DE
28 November 2022

16276299R00024